MW01230417

HEALTHY ALKALINE DIET RECIPES FOR BEGINNERS

An Essential Guide to Destroy 12Lbs of Fat, Maintain Health, Stay Active and Liver Longer with 25+ Mouth-Watering, Simple, and Quick Alkaline Diet Recipes for Beginners to Control PH Level in Body.

BY

Madge Weaver

Table of Contents

INTRODUCTION

Alkaline diet (otherwise called the alkaline debris diet, alkaline corrosive diet, corrosive debris diet, and corrosive alkaline diet) portrays a gathering of approximately related diets dependent on the misinterpretation that various sorts of food can affect the pH equilibrium of the body. It started from the corrosive debris speculation, which fundamentally identified with osteoporosis research. Defenders of the diet accept that specific food varieties can influence the acridity (pH) of the body and that the adjustment of pH can accordingly be utilized to treat or forestall illness. Solid labs have done broad exploration regarding this matter and have proven the hypothesis according to the guaranteed system of this diet. Because of proof, it is suggested by dietitians or other wellbeing experts.

1.   Grilled Vegetable Pesto Pasta

prep time: 20 MINUTES cook time: 15 MINUTES
total time: 35 MINUTES

ingredients:

- Pesto
- 1 cup of basil leaves
- 3 tbsp crude hemp hearts
- 1/4 c pine nuts and additionally crude pecans, or crude cashews
- 1/4c olive oil and touch for consistency
- 1 clove garlic squashed
- squeeze ocean salt

- Method-mix well in blender or food processor. (I once in a while twofold this and freeze half for a speedy dinner next time around)
- Pasta
- 1 pkg earthy colored rice penne noodles,
- 1 tsp ocean salt
- Method-bubble pasta for approx 15 mins and throw with pesto to your ideal consistency.
- Veggies
- veggies arranged enormous bowl of an assortment of new natural veggies chopped generally – I utilize 4-5 sweet peppers, 2 onions, 3 sm zucchini, 4 carrots, 1-2 sm eggplant, 1 pack asparagus-what at any point suits your extravagant!
- approx 3tbsp additional virgin olive oil
- 2 tsp ocean salt
- cherry tomatoes-optional (added toward the end for only a couple minutes)

Method:

1. throw veggies with olive oil and ocean salt at that point fill bar-b-que flame broil dish, barbecue veggies till they are marginally

delicate and slightly burned. At last, throw simmered veggies with the pesto pasta. Season with ocean salt to taste and present with a major green serving of mixed greens. This is yummy even at room temperature so can be made a small piece a head of time. Appreciate extras the following day-that is if there are any! (Tip: this is one of those suppers you could make prior in the day and afterward transport to the sea shore for supper with basic greens threw with a light dressing.) Enjoy!

2. Alkaline Style Lemon Pesto Salmon, Cashew Ceasar, Broccolini Chop

Total: 1 hr 5 min Prep: 20 min Cook: 45 min

Cashew Ceasar

Ingredients:

- 1 head of romaine lettuce washed and chopped
- 1/2 c olive oil
- 1 tbsp hemp nuts
- 2 tsp crude sesame seed tahini
- tbsp braggs fluid aminos
- 1/2 little zucchini stripped and generally chopped (approx. 1 cup)
- 1 clove new garlic
- 3 tbsp new lemon juice

- spot of celtic ocean salt

Method

- Join all ingredients with the exception of lettuce in Blender, scratch drawbacks and blend well, adding extra shower of olive oil if necessary for consistency.
- For the Cashew Croutons
- 1/2 c crude cashew nuts
- 1/4 tsp of celtic ocean salt
- 1 clove garlic squashed
- 1 tbsp olive oil

Method

- •Place all ingredients in little saute skillet and saute until cashew are gently seared. Spot in little serving bowl and put away.
- •When salmon is done on the BBQ prepare salad and offer cashew bread garnishes for visitors at the table
- Broccolini Chop
- yield: 6 servings (approx 3/4 c each)
- 5 cups broccolini chopped into to 1" computers
- 1 tbsp celtic ocean salt
- 4 tbsp crude sesame seeds
- 2 tbsp crude sesame oil

- 1 tsp toasted sesame oil
- tbsp braggs fluid aminos

Method

- •Lightly toast sesame seeds in saute prospect few moments observe near abstain from consuming, put away.
- •Combine both sesame oils, and braggs, put away.
- •Bring enormous pot of water to bubble, add ocean salt, (when salmon is done is an ideal opportunity to cook brocolini) and afterward cook broccolini for max 2 minutes. Channel and spot in serving dish.
- •Drizzle sesame-braggs blend over broccolini and tenderly throw. Sprinkle with sesame seeds and serve.
- *Note For Raw Foodies: Massage the broccolini for 3-5 mins and throw in dressing-season w/ocean salt whenever wanted.
- Lemon Pesto Salmon
- Yield: 6 servings
- 6 filets of wild salmon with skin on
- 2-12" long cedar board splashed for 30-60 mins in water (it could be sliced into 6

computers preceding dousing whenever wanted for serving)

- 1/4 cups generally chopped parsley
- juice of one lemon juice
- zing of 1 lemon
- 2 cloves garlic generally chopped
- 3 tbsp olive oil + chomped more for consistency if necessary
- squeeze ocean salt
- 1/2 c crude nuts (pine, pecan or cashew or a blend) I've attempted them all with incredible achievement!
- sugar 2-3 drops fluid stevia or 2 tsp agave

Method:

1. Combine all ingredients in a blender or food processor, scratching down and joining until all around blended and of a pleasant surface, not pureed. Pesto ought not be runny, however thick and finished.

2. Prepare the salmon by washing and wiping off. Eliminate cedar board from dousing tub and delicately wipe surface off. Spot salmon on board skin side down.

3. Spread pesto liberally on the top surface of the fish. Spot planked fish on pre-warmed bar-b-que flame broil with top shut and barbecue until it chips and a spread blade embedded in focus parcel is hot when eliminated approx 10-20 mins relying upon size and thickness of fish.

4. Remove from barbecue and afterward from board and permit to several minutes while cooking the broccolini and preparing the plate of mixed greens.

3. Mediterranean Layered Dip

Prep Time 10 minutes   Total Time 10 minutes

Mediterranean layered dip:

- Approx 6 cups – enough for a military! This will take care of a huge gathering at a social affair when combined with a liberal crudites platter
- 1 16 ounces cherry tomatoes quartered and put away
- 10 basil leaves chopped finely, put away
- 1/3 cup pine nuts
- 1 cup simmered peppers – optionally one can utilize bumped broiled peppers or take 2 huge red peppers diced and threw with olive oil and

celtic ocean salt, and meal on material paper at 375 for 20 mins. Cool and put away.

- Lentil and Kalamata Olive Spread – Bottom Layer
- 1/2 cup dried earthy colored lentils cooked in 1 cup of water
- 1/2 cup pitted kalamata olives
- 1/3 cup additional virgin olive oil + extra for consistency
- 1 clove garlic
- 1/4 tsp salt
- 1/4 cup chopped parsley

Method.

- Spot lentils in water and bring to bubble, at that point lessen warmth to low and stew for approx 20-25 mins until delicate and the vast majority of the water is retained. Channel and spot in bowl of food processor. Add remaining ingredients to food processor. Mix until altogether joined with a slight surface, adding extra sprinkle of oil if necessary. Spoon blend into the lower part of your layering dish. Wash food processor. Make the following plunge.
- Rich Basil Dip – Second Layer

- 1/2 cups cashews, drenched for approx 60 minutes
- 1/2 cup diced zucchini
- 2 tbsp chopped shallot
- 1/4 tsp ocean salt
- 1 clove garlic chopped
- 1/3 cup new basil leaves
- 1/4 cup new parsley
- 1/4 cup olive oil
- 1 tbsp new lemon juice
- 2 tbsp separated water + extra for consistency

Method
- Spot all ingredients into bowl of food processor and mix until smooth and rich, adding some extra sifted water for consistency if necessary. Spoon equitably on top of the lentil and olive layer. Wash food processor and make the following plunge.
- White Bean Dip w/Rosemary – Final Dip Layer
- 2 14 oz tins of cannellini beans, drained and flushed - natural if conceivable
- 1 clove garlic
- 1 enormous branch rosemary, leaves eliminated from stem

- 1/4 tsp ocean salt
- 1/3 cup olive oil + sprinkle more for consistency

Method:

1. Spot above ingredients in food processor with S edge and heartbeat to join. Mood killer processor, scratch disadvantages of bowl and afterward mix again until joined. Add extra oil whenever needed to make a spreadable consistency that isn't dry however gently finished and velvety. Season to taste with additional salt whenever wanted.

2. To complete the layering, spread the cooked peppers on the velvety basil layer. Next spoon the white bean plunge liberally on top of the peppers spreading cautiously. Presently top with chopped tomatoes, trailed by basil lastly the pine nuts. Doesn't it look pretty?

3. Present with brilliant veggies sticks, for example, jicama, red peppers, delicately whitened asparagus, cucumber sticks or your different top picks. Appreciate:)

4. Raw Chocolate Truffles

Prep Time: 20 minutes Total Time: 20 minutes
Crude Hazelnut Truffles:

- Approx 20 truffles
- 1/2 cups crude cacao powder
- 1/3 to 1/2 cup natural agave syrup (conform as you would prefer)
- 3 drops fluid stevia-optional
- 1/4 tsp ground vanilla or liquor free fluid vanilla
- spot of Himalayan salt
- 1/2 cup crude hazelnuts doused approx 2-3 hours, drained

- 1/4 cup crude cashews doused approx 2-3 hours, drained
- 1 tsp hazelnut oil-optional
- 1/3 cup crude natural coconut oil
- 1/3 cup cocoa margarine, finely chopped
- 1 formula of crude plunging chocolate-see beneath

Method
- Get ready and measure out with or without ingredients and set.
- Spot cocoa margarine in a twofold evaporator dish over bubbling water to dissolve the cocoa spread for 1-2 mins. Eliminate from heat before every one of the pieces have softened leaving the top dish over the boiling water and afterward add the coconut oil to the dissolved cocao spread permitting it to liquefy.
- Add any remaining ingredients to bowl of food processor and afterward add the oils and cycle quickly until smooth and velvety, framing a hefty blend. Utilizing spatula, scratch blend into a bowl and chill for approx 45 mins.
- Whenever combination is chilled, scoop by storing teaspoon fulls and fold into balls and

chill again for at any rate 10 mins on a material lined plate. These would now be able to be dunked into the fluid chocolate-formula is underneath or folded into crude cacao powder or fine dried coconut.

- Coconut Cashew Truffles
- Yield: 12-16 truffles
- 1/4 cup natural agave syrup
- 1/4 cup natural crude coconut oil
- 1/2 cup finely destroyed natural crude dried coconut
- 1/2 cup crude natural cashews, doused approx 2-3 hours, drained
- 1/4 tsp ground vanilla or liquor free fluid vanilla
- pleasant spot of Himalayan salt
- Method
- Spot all ingredients with the exception of coconut oil in food processor. Liquefy coconut oil either in a glass estimating cup set in hot faucet water for 5 mins or over a twofold heater for only 1 moment or less. It liquefies effectively and rapidly.
- Add to combination and blend until very much consolidated, scratching a few times.

Combination may shape a ball. Utilizing spatula scratch combination into a bowl and chill for approx 45 mins. Whenever blend is chilled, scoop by piling teaspoon fulls and fold into balls and chill again for in any event 10 mins on a material lined plate. These would now be able to be plunged into the fluid chocolate-formula is beneath or folded into crude cacao powder or fine dried coconut.

- Plunging Chocolate
- Yield: enough chocolate to plunge approx 24-30 truffles
- 1 cup cacao margarine, finely chopped
- 1/2 cups crude cacao powder
- 1/4 cup agave syrup or less-conform to taste
- touch of Himalayan salt
- 1/4 tsp ground vanilla or liquor free fluid vanilla

Method:

1. Spot cacao margarine in a twofold kettle container over bubbling water shower to soften the cocoa spread for 1-2 mins. Eliminate from heat before every one of the pieces have liquefied. Add remaining ingredients to the

skillet and mix until smooth, at that point eliminate from water shower.

2. Take one kind of truffles from ice chest and spot a toothpick in each. Plunge every one into the fluid chocolate permitting the abundance to run off, at that point setting the truffle on a plate fixed with material or wax paper.

3. At the point when all are plunged cautiously eliminate the toothpicks by winding and tenderly pulling upward. To cover the toothpick opening add an enhancement of a nut by plunging the nut in chocolate barely enough to make it stay on tops or spot fine destroyed coconut or cacao nibs on the highest point of each before the chocolate solidifies.

4. On the off chance that the plunging chocolate turns out to be too thick you may put it over the heated water briefly. When all truffles are plunged you can accelerate the solidifying interaction by chilling for a small piece say 10 mins.

5. Try not to leave them in the cooler excessively long as they will shape buildup when eliminated from the cold and this will leave an undesirable completion on the outside of the

chocolate. In the event that you run out of plunging chocolate you can roll the truffle places in cocoa powder or fine dried coconut. Presto, you have elite chocolates now!

5. Asian Pear & Green Apple Raw Tart Apple Cream

Prep: 20 mins Cook: 40 mins Total: 1 hr

Asian Pear and Green Apple Raw Tart Apple Cream:

- Serves Approx 6-8
- For the Cashew Apple Cream
- 1 cup crude cashews, doused for 30-60 mins
- 1 green apple cored and chopped
- juice of 1/2 lemon
- 5-7 tbsp sifted (soluble) water (add the last 2 tbsp just if necessary)
- 1 tbsp agave syrup or use part stevia fluid drops (a mix of both is pleasant and diminishes the agave sum)

Method

- Spot all ingredients in blender or food cycle and mix until fine and rich scratching drawbacks to consolidate well. Move to a little bowl and refrigerate while planning tart outside layer. This combination is soooo scrumptious spooned over the tart or sprinkled from a press bottle maybe as a pleasant example on the highest point of the tart.
- For the Tart Shell
- 1/2 cups walnuts, doused 60 mins
- 1/2 cup crude almonds, doused 60 mins
- 8 delicate dried natural dates, pitts eliminated
- 1/4 tsp nutmeg, newly ground nutmeg on the off chance that you can
- squeeze ground cloves
- 2 tsp ground cinnamon
- 1 tsp vanilla
- 1 tbsp almond oil, or other nut oil
- 1 - 2 tbsp sifted water, if necessary for joining the abovementioned

Method

- Join all ingredients aside from the water in food processor mixing with S sharp edge until the mass starts to bunch together adding the water if necessary to consolidate the blend taking after the picture beneath. Press blend into a tart container of decision (fluted 10" round or oval) or free structure a tart with somewhat of a lip to hold a shallow layer of filling. Chill the outside while you set up the filling.

- For the Pear and Apple Filling
- 1 huge Asian pear
- 2 green apples
- juice of 1/2 lemon
- 1/2 to 1 tsp ground cinnamon
- spot of nutmeg, newly ground nutmeg in the event that you can
- touch of allspice
- 1 tbsp agave syrup

Methods:

1. Crush lemon juice into medium estimated bowl. Utilizing a mandolin or your blade abilities, finely dice the Asian pear and apple taking after the picture beneath, setting in bowl of lemon juice, covering as you cleave. Add flavors and agave syrup and mix. Permit

to stand 10 mins, at that point strain off the fluid and put something aside for your smoothie tomorrow!

2. To finish the tart spoon the filling into the tart shell, evening out it, spending all the filling. Top with finely sliced apple. Appreciate!

3. Tart is best eaten same day yet will keep in the ice chest for a couple of days.

6.   Healthy Alkaline Salad dressings

Prep: 10 mins Cook: 10 mins Total:Per dressing 20 mins

Chive Dressing Simple Salad:

- salad for two
- 1 nice head of your favourite lettuce, I chose butter lettuce, sliced in half lengthwise
- 1 avocado, halved and sliced, some for dressing, remainder for salad
- 3 chive flowers, two for garnish, one for dressing
- few cherry tomatoes, sliced in half
- for the dressing
- 1/3 cup olive oil
- juice of one half lemon

- 1/4 tsp fine Himilayan sea salt
- 1/4 tsp braggs liquid aminos
- 1/4 avocado
- 2 tbsp sunflower seeds, soaked for 10-15 mns
- 4 tbsp filtered water
- 2 tbsp chopped fresh chives, 1 fresh chive flower

Method

- Lets start with the dressing so the flavours can mingle while you prep the salad. Soak sunflower seeds in filtered water for at least 10 mins. Then place remaining ingredients in blender and combine till creamy. Check for seasoning and let rest. Place lettuce halves on two plates ,add avocado and tomato. Garnish with chive flowers, arugula flowers and drizzle with dressing, offering additional dressing when you serve.
- Mexican Salad Dressing
- Yield: 1 cup dressing
- 1/2 cup olive oil
- 2 tbsp flax oil-optional
- 1 tbsp hemp oil-optional
- 2 tablespoons fresh lime juice

- 2 tbsp lemon juice
- 2 tbsp agave syrup
- 1/2 tablespoon celtic salt or sea salt
- 1 – 2 cloves minced garlic
- 1/4 cup chopped fresh cilantro
- 1/2 tablespoon ground cumin
- 1 tsp ground black pepper
- 1 teaspoon chili powder
- cayenne pepper to season at serving time

Method

- Wisk together and let stand 10 mins before serving. Great for any salad with beans and greens.
- Lime & Ginger Salad Dressing
- Yield: 3/4 cup dressing
- juice of 1/2 lemon
- juice of 2 limes
- 1/3c sunflower oil
- fresh very finely grated ginger
- 1/2tsp honey dijon mustard
- pinch salt
- pinch of fresh ground pepper

- sweeten with agave til desired- approx 1-2 tbsp.-using a 2 drops of stevia in combination will reduce your amount of agave.

Method

- Combine all ingredients and shake or wisk and store in refrigerator for up to 3 days. This sweet lime dressing is lovely with any greens and adding things like mango or papaya with avocado and some nuts (I have even added shrimp) is really nice and will certainly impress guests. You can bump up the omegas in this by adding a 1-2 tablespoons of flax oil or hemp oil or even Udo's 3-6-9 Omega oil. Always taste your omega oils first before adding to a dressing so you know if they will complement the flavour. Once I had a lemon flavoured omega oil and didn't realize and it didn't mix with the flavours I was creating- kinda messed up my plan.
- Triple Citrus Dressing
- Yield: 1 cup dressing
- juice of 1 large grapefruit
- juice of 1 navel orange
- juice of 1 large lemon

- 1/3 c raw cold pressed sunflower oil (or flax or olive oil or a combination)
- 1 1/2 tbsp agave syrup – or to taste
- 1/4 tsp honey mustard
- pinch of Celtic sea salt
- 1/4 tsp fresh grated ginger

Method

- Combine the above ingredients in a measuring cup and wisk well. Great with greens, avocado slices, grapefruit, walnuts and a stack of sprouts on top.
- Ceasar Dressing
- yield: 1 1/2 cups dressing
- 1/2 c olive oil
- 1 tbsp hemp nuts
- 2 tsp raw sesame seed tahini
  - tbsp braggs liquid aminos
- 1/2 small zucchini peeled and roughly chopped (approx. 1 cup)
- 1 clove fresh garlic
- 3 tbsp fresh lemon juice
- pinch of celtic sea salt

Method

- Combine all ingredients in blender, scrape down sides and mix well, adding additional drizzle of olive oil if needed for consistency. Best on romain but nice on mixed garden salad too.
- Asian Dressing, great for coleslaws
- yield: 1/2 cup dressing
- 2 tbsp braggs liquid aminos
- 2 tbsp extra virgin olive oil-cold pressed organic if possible
- juice of 1/2 lemon
- 1 tbsp toasted sesame oil
- 2 teaspoons grated ginger
- 2 tsp raw sesame tahini
- Celtic sea salt to taste
- Method
- Wisk all dressing ingredients together in a measuring cup.
- Ginger & Hemp Dressing—My all time Fave- considered liquid gold!
- Yield: approx 1 cup
- juice of 1.5 lemons
- 1/2 c extra virgin olive oil-cold pressed
- 3 tbsp Udo's oil (or more if you like)
- 1 tbsp tahini -preferably raw

- 2 tbsp braggs liquid aminos
- 1 tbsp filtered water
- 1/3 c hemp nuts
- 1 tsp finely grated ginger

Method

- Blend all ingredients well in a high speed blender, scraping down sides to incorporate. Pour into a salad dressing bottle and enjoy. This dressing will keep well for up to 3 days if it lasts that long! My 5 yr old daughter has been known to drink it! This is great on any mixed veggie salad.
- Thai Sweet & Sour dressing
- Yield: approx 5/8 cup
- 3 3/4 tbsp fresh squeezed lime juice (approx 1 large lime)
- 4 garlic cloves,minced or crushed
- 4 1/2 tbsp braggs liquid aminos
- 1 tbsp agave syrup
  - 1/2 tsp finely minced jalapeno pepper

Method

- In a measuring cup mix all dressing ingredients well, test for balance of sweet, salty, sour and spicy, then let stand 5-10 mins for flavours to meld. Best with this salad recipe.

- Creamy Lemon Pepper Dressing
- yield: approx 1 cup
- 1/2 cup diced peeled zucchini
- 1/3 cup raw Brazil nuts
- 1/3 cup extra virgin olive oil
- juice and zest of one lemon
- 1 very small garlic clove
- 1/2 tsp agave
- 1/4 tsp Himalayan sea salt
- 1/4 tsp fresh ground black pepper
- Method Place all ingredients into blender and combine well. For consistency you may add a tbsp of filtered water if needed. I rather like it thick and creamy but it will further thicken because of the nuts. Nice with walnuts, grapefruit and greens.
- Sweet Slaw Dressing, great with peppers & jicama
- Yield: Approx 3/4 cup
- 1/2 cup cilantro, chopped or snipped
- juice of one lime, approx 3 tbsp
- 1/4 cup extra virgin olive oil
- 2 tbsp agave syrup

- 1 large clove garlic, crushed
- 1/2 tsp cumin
- 1/4 tsp cayenne or to taste
- 1/8 tsp sea salt

Method

- To allow flavours to mingle, prepare dressing first by combining cilantro lime juice, olive oil, agave, garlic and spices. Stir well and set aside. If you wish, the agave can be replaced partly or completely with approx 1/3 cup fresh pressed apple juice as a sweetener.
- Chipotle Dip or Dressing
- Yield: Approx 1 1/2 cups
- 1 cup raw almonds, soaked 30-60 mins if you have time
- 1/4 to 1/2 tsp chipotle pepper spice, the more, the hotter
- 1 1/4 tsp smoked paprika
- 1 clove garlic crushed
- 3 tbsp fresh squeezed lemon juice
- 1/2 cup filtered water
- 2 tbsp olive oil
- 1/2 tsp Celtic sea salt

Method:

1. Combine above ingredients in blender and combine til creamy and smooth, adding 1-2 tbsp additional water for consistency only if needed. Use as spread inside wraps and serve extra along side cuz it's sooo yummy!   This makes a nice salad dressing if you thin this a wee bit more with either almond milk or additional water.
2. Creamy Mint & Lime Dressing
3. Yield: Approx 1 1/4 cups
4. 1/4 cup extra virgin olive oil
5. juice & zest of one fresh lime
6. juice of 1/2 lemon
7. 5 stems fresh mint, leaves and stems
8. 1/2 avocado
9. 2 tsp agave or as you may (1 tsp with 3 drops liquid stevia)
10. pinch sea salt
11. 2-3 tbsp filtered water for consistency
12. Method Place all ingredients in a blender. and combine until mint is pureed.
13. Creamy Sesame Sauce
14. Yield: Approx 1 3/4 cups-makes a lot!
15. 3/4 cup tahini, preferrably raw but either will do in a pinch

16. 1/4 cup braggs liquid aminos

17. 1 tsp freshly grated ginger, optional

18. juice of 1-2 lemons or 1/4 cup

19. 1/2 tsp toasted sesame oil, optional (this isn't raw)

20. 1-2 tbsp filtered water

21. Method Combine ingredients except water in a measuring cup and stir well, adding filtered water a bit at a time until smooth and creamy. Thin to desired consistency.

7. Raw Coconut Cream Pie 'n Berries

Prep Time: 20 min Total Time: 20 min

Raw Coconut Cream Pie 'n Berries:

- 10-12 servings
- For the Crust
- 2 1/4 cups dried destroyed natural coconut
- 1/3 cup additional virgin coconut oil
- 2 dates, pitts eliminated
- tbsp maple syrup
- 1 tbsp liquor free natural vanilla
- cups finely diced natural strawberries, to line the hull

Method

- Spot all ingredients, with the exception of strawberries, in a food processor and join well until coconut oil is uniformly conveyed and the combination is starting to tie together. To guarantee simple expulsion of pie from container, you may cut a plate of material paper and spot in lower part of pie place. Scoop outside layer combination into a profound 10"pie plate. With a spoon, delicately allot the blend up the sides of the skillet, directing it toward the top however not pushing down until the combination is equally disseminated. At that point utilizing the rear of the spoon, press combination down and smooth out the surfaces guaranteeing no openings in the hull approx 1/4" thick. Chill for 30-60 mins. Spread diced strawberries on the lower part of the hull not long prior to pouring the filling in.
- For the filling
- 2 cups youthful coconut meat (approx 2 coconuts opened, scooped and diced)
- 1/2 cup diced, stripped small zucchini
- 1/2 cup cashews, splashed 30 mins and drained

- 1/3 cup virgin coconut oil-the best oil you can manage!
- 1/4 cups new youthful coconut water (from 1-2 coconuts relying upon size)
- 1/2 tbsp liquor free natural vanilla
- 2 tbsp maple syrup or to taste
- 6 strawberries sliced, for beautifying the top
- 6 raspberries, for beautifying the top
- new mint branches, for beautifying the top

Method:

1. Spot all ingredients (with the exception of berries and mint) in a blender and cycle until smooth, more than once scratching sides down to support total blending, arriving at a smooth, plush, velvety combination that is still thick. Abstain from adding more dampness and continue on the off chance that it is thick to keep a solidness that will make the end-product hold together well. In the event that you have a Vitamix utilize the poker that embeds in the top. A blender appeared to arrive at a much smoother mass than a food processor however analyze on the off chance that you may. Fill strawberry lined chilled

covering. Chill 4 hours or over night. Instantly prior to serving, finish the firm pie surface cautiously (make an effort not to move your cuts in the wake of putting them down as it might stamp the surface) with the sliced strawberries, raspberries and mint according to picture (headings underneath) or in your own innovative way. Appreciate:)

8. Creamy Cannellini Bean Sauce over Spelt

Prep Time 10 minutes Cook Time 35 minutes

Total Time 45 minutes

Rich Cannellini Bean Sauce over Spelt Fettucini, Summer Green Beans and Peppers:

- Serves 6-8, close by a green serving of mixed greens
- ingredients
- pk spelt fettucini noodles, yielding approx 4 cups cooked noodles
- 10 cloves garlic, divided
- 3tbsp additional virgin olive oil + 1/4c
- 1-14 oz tin cannellini beans, drained and washed
- 1/2 tsp new rosemary, chopped

- 1/4 – 1/3 c unsweetened almond milk
- 1 tbsp new lemon juice
- 1 tbsp + 1/4 tsp celtic ocean salt
- 1 lb new green beans, sliced longwise and fifty-fifty
- 1 huge bundle slender asparagus lances, cut in 1/2 (if fat cut length astute)
- red peppers, cut into 1/4' slender strips
- pistachio beating

Method:

1. Set up all veggies and spot in liner container all set over a pot of water. Try not to steam yet.

2. Fill another huge pot with water, add 1 tbsp celtic ocean salt, and spot over high warmth, prepared for pasta.

3. In a little saute container add garlic and 3 tbsp olive oil and cautiously saute over medium warmth for 3-5 mins until garlic is delicate or clear, at that point eliminate from warmth to cool to some degree.

4. Spot cannellini beans, sauteed garlic in oil, + 1/4 cup extra oil, rosemary, lemon juice, and 1/4 tsp ocean salt in blender, measure until sleek. Change preparing on a case by case basis or thickness with additional almond milk, yielding a substantial however pourable sauce.

5. Presently add pasta to bubbling water, cook as coordinated might be approx 8-10 mins.

6. Steam veggies for just 3-4 mins once water is bubbling and delivering steam-don't over cook, they should in any case be firm however marginally delicate.

7. Channel pasta and spot in enormous serving dish, adding steamed veggies and afterward delicately pour creamed bean sauce over and throw cautiously, yet completely.

8. Present with squashed pistachio besting. See note underneath.

Pistachio Topping:

1/2 cup crude pistachios, delicately toasted or not, better crude, yet you choose

1/8 tsp fine ocean salt

squeeze stew pieces

finely ground zing of 1/4 lemon

Spot all ingredients in blender or food cycle and granulate until chopped however not totally uniform. Use as fixing for pastas, rice or plates of mixed greens.

9. Marinated Kale Roasted Veggies

PREP TIME 10 mins TOTAL TIME 10 mins 2 lg

plates or 4 little plates

Ingredient:

- medications yam, 1/2" diced
- 1 huge beet, 1/2" diced
- 1 onion, 1/2" diced
- tbsp coconut oil, softened
- sprinkle of fine Himalayan salt
- 5 cups kale, ribs eliminated and finely chopped into little reduced down pieces
- juice of 1 lime
- tbsp of additional virgin olive oil
- 1 avocado, pitted and diced
- 1/4 tsp chipotle chile pepper zest (or to taste)
- 1/2 tsp smoked paprika

- 1/4 tsp Himalayan salt
- 2-3 drops stevia or 1 tsp maple syrup

Method:

1. Preheat oven to 350F. Throw yam with a shower of the softened coconut oil (I typically pop a warmth evidence custard dish in the oven for a couple of mins to dissolve the oil) and a sprinkle of salt and pour onto one finish of a heating sheet fixed with material paper. Rehash with onions and pour close by the potatoes in a touch of pile so they will cook a little more slow that the rest, and do likewise with the beets and pour them toward the finish of the plate. This all appears to be fastidious however keeps the beets from shading the whole clump of veggies pink. Feel free to combine them all as one on the off chance that you wouldn't fret the dying:) Roast the diced veggies for 30 mins or until fork delicate. Then, place lemon and olive oil into a huge profound bowl and back rub utilizing your hands for around brief at that point add (have somebody help you on the off chance that you would prefer not to wash your hands) remaining

ingredients and back rub till the avocado is totally creamed through the greens and the greens have mellowed fairly, approx 1-2 mins. Separation onto plates and top with cooked veggies (I permitted the veggies to cool a piece prior to garnish the greens to try not to warm the greens by any means). Presto, appreciate!

2. ps. A special reward to this formula is an awesome hand treatment! Avocado rubbed into your hands makes them overall quite delicate! Make sure to eliminate any jewelery or rings before hand to try not to grime them up. Lastly, the kale is more delicate the following day obviously subsequent to marinating over night.

10. Ginger Creamed Pecans & Chopped Kale

Total Time: 20 Minutes Yield 1 huge serving of mixed greens

Ingredients:

- 1/2 cup walnuts, doused for the time being ideally or min 30-60 mins in any event
- 1/4 c additional virgin olive oil
- 2 tbsp new lemon juice
- 1/4 cup sifted water
- 1/2 tbsp newly ground ginger
- tbsp green onion, utilize the white parts for the most part
- spot of Himalayan or celtic salt
- 8 drops stevia or optionally 4 drops os stevia in addition to 1 tsp coconut nectar

- cups kale, very much chopped into little scaled down laptops
- 1 cup red cabbage, daintily shaved
- 1/4 of one pomelo, stripped and layers eliminated
- radishes, daintily sliced
- 1/2 avocado, sliced

Method:

1. Lets start with the dressing so it can rest and assemble it's flavors. Spot doused walnuts, olive oil, lemon juice, water, new ginger, green onion, salt, and stevia/coconut nectar into blender. Interaction combination, scratching drawbacks until a rich blend is reached. Fill a serving dish and put away.

2. Then, hack the kale and spot in your serving bowl. Include the finely sliced cabbage and throw delicately. Top with pomelo, walnuts, radish and avocado. Pour dressing over salad liberally and prepare well. Dive in or then again permit it to rest 5 mins or more to relax the kale fairly. Appreciate. Get serious about this formula on the off chance that you are in good company or you could share:)

3. Kale Pomelo and Pecan salad (1 of 7)

4. Remember this plate of mixed greens is considered antacid adjusted, not simply soluble as it has the pomelo and the walnuts that are on the low acidic side balancing this serving of mixed greens to about 85% basic to 15% acidic.

5. In the event that you are at present not well perhaps avoid the pomelo and it's sugar content (sugar angers an acidic body) this time and take the plunge with simply the kale business and vanquish the soluble landscape so you can be well once more. In the event that you are recuperating feel free to join a modest quantity of nutrient C rich pomelo to fortify and assemble your invulnerability once more. It's no pleasant inclination sick so in the event that you can adhere to the most elevated proportion of basic food varieties you can and you'll have returned to your sound dynamic self instantly.

6. In the event that you have depended on a remedy remember that you should detox the result of synthetic compounds from your framework so by and by a clean soluble eating

regimen will work well for you. A probiotic supplement might be all together also on the off chance that you had an anti-toxin as a solution to aid restoring a reasonable gut vegetation (stomach related track) that will help evade likely yeast/candida issues.

11. Alkaline Slaw with Pomegranate, Salted Caramel Pecans & Starfruit

PREP TIME: 20 MINUTES TOTAL TIME: 20 MINUTES Yield: Serves a horde of 12-15 as a side dish or less as a fundamental

Ingredients:

- Salted Caramel Pecans
- 2 tbsp olive oil
- 4 tsp lucuma powder + 1 tsp
- 6 drops stevia
- 1/8 tsp fine Himalyan salt + more to taste if necessary
- great scramble of cinnamon

- tsp maple syrup
- cups crude walnut parts
- Ginger Lime Dressing
- juice of two limes
- 1/2 cup of additional virgin olive oil
- 1 tbsp newly ground ginger + more to taste whenever wanted
- 8-10 drop stevia
- 1 tbsp maple syrup
- salt and pepper
- Slaw
- 1 napa cabbage, finely sliced
- 1/4 little white cabbage, finely sliced
- 1/2 cup of finely chopped mint leaves + a couple for embellish
- 1 enormous pomegranate, cultivated
- 1 star organic product, sliced

Method:

1. Lets start with the nuts so they can rest and retain a portion of the flavors. In a medium estimated bowl add the oil and the 3 tsp of lucuma and wisk until smooth. Add the stevia, salt and cinnamon and mix well. Add the teaspoon of maple syrup and mix delicately to

consolidate. This will thicken and get smooth however could seize up in the event that you over mix. Add the walnuts and throw truly well to cover. Presently sprinkle with the additional teaspoon of lucuma to dry the nuts out a small piece. Taste and check for an equilibrium of pungent to sweet and add more salt if necessary or another drop of stevia (and afterward throw like crazee to disseminate). Presently... put them away and STOP eating them!

2. Next make the dressing. Wisk every one of the ingredients, taste for an equilibrium of tart and sweet and change if necessary. I luv heaps of ginger so add more in the event that you like. Put away so flavors can blend.

3. Presently shred the cabbages, cleave the mint, and seed the pomegranate. Consolidate these treats in a huge serving of mixed greens bowl however save a couple pomegrate seeds to decorate. Tenderly throw in the walnuts additionally saving some to sprinkle on the top. Presently lets extravagant up the top and add the sliced star organic product, the pomegrate seeds, walnuts and a couple of more mint

leaves. Throw with the dressing just prior to serving. Taa daa! Kindly note that this plate of mixed greens is best that very day however genuinely... I altogether appreciated the smidgen of extras daily later.

4. Assuredly you can sub different nuts instead of the walnuts like pecans maybe yet the walnuts as of now have a carmel-ish flavor. Pecans are decent, I attempted them excessively however somewhat more harsh so you need to improve somewhat extra. These two nuts have pleasant fissure to trap the covering. In any case, I am right now testing by getting dried out a group of these nuts utilizing each nut I had from hazelnuts to cashews and almonds for a blended nibble over the special times of year. I'll tell you how they end up. They may be much more pleasant on this serving of mixed greens. You simply need time to get dried out.

12. Fiddle Heads with Creamy Kamut Orzo & Spring Peas

Total: 35 minActive: 35 min Yield: Serves 6-8 as a dish to go with a pleasant green plate of mixed greens

Ingredients1:

- 1/2 cups kamut orzo pasta
- 2 cups new or frozen peas
- huge white onion, diced
- 1 tbsp virgin coconut oil
- garlic cloves, minced
- 1 tin incredible northern beans or cannellini beans, drained and washed or 1/2 cups cooked dried white beans

- 1/2 cup unsweetened almond milk
- a press of new lemon
- 1/4-1/2 tsp ocean salt + more for water
- 40 fiddleheads, around, washed and scoured
- additional virgin olive oil
- touch of brittle ocean salt, as Malden Flakes.

Method:

1. Put two medium pots of water on to bubble, both all around salted with about a tablespoon of ocean salt.

2. In the mean time, sauté onion in coconut oil till clear cover 5-7 mins, adding 2 cloves of minced garlic in the last 2 mins. Move half of this combination to a blender and empty the rest of a medium estimated blending bowl and put away.

3. Add orzo to bubbling water and cook according to headings on pkg (approx 8-10mins) adding frozen peas throughout the previous 2 minutes.

4. Steam fiddleheads for 10-12 mins until delicate. Channel and run cool water over to prevent them from cooking any further. Throw

fiddleheads in a shower of additional virgin olive oil and a sprinkle of ocean salt.

5. In blender, add beans and almond milk and cycle until velvety, adding the last minced clove of garlic and lemon press and preparing only a couple seconds more.

6. Channel orzo and peas and fill blending bowl in with onion, at that point cover with velvety beans.

7. Serve orzo finished off with 4-6 fiddleheads. Trimming with new chives or other new spices as you may and a disintegrate of ocean salt.

8. Appreciate:)

13. Healthy Lectin-Free Vegan Chocolate Mousse

prep 5 mins active 24 hourstotal 24 hours, 5 mins yield 1 cup

Ingredients:

- would organic be able to full-fat coconut milk (13.5 ounce can)
- 1 tablespoon natural crude cacao powder
- tablespoons natural crude granular sweetener*
- *Lectin-Free: Use non-GMO xylitol or stevia mix

Guidelines

Progressed Preparation:

1. Put a jar of full-fat coconut milk toward the rear of your fridge - at any rate 24 hours, or more, prior to

making this formula. The "fat" in the can should be strong to make the mousse.

2. Eliminate the jar of coconut milk from the fridge. The top portion of the can ought to be the solidified coconut "fat" and the base half ought to be fluid coconut "water".

3. Scoop out the solidified "fat" a piece of the coconut milk from the highest point of the can and add it to the bowl of your blender. Save the coconut "water" to add to a smoothie.

4. Add your preferred cacao powder and sugar to the blender bowl and blend on fast with a whisk connection until it pinnacles and transforms into a soft mousse.

5. Optional: Top with crude cacao nibs, raspberries, strawberries, scaled down chocolate chips (not sans lectin), destroyed coconut, and so forth

6. Store in the fridge in a water/air proof sans bpa holder until prepared to serve or it will get delicate whenever forgotten about at room temperature.

7. Appreciate!

14. Lectin-Free Vegan Cheesy Oven Baked Mushrooms

prep 5 minscook 20 minstotal 25 mins

Ingredients:

- For the flavoring:
- 1/2 cup almond flour
- 1/2 cup healthful yeast
- 1/4 - 1/2 teaspoon natural ground cayenne pepper
- 1/2 teaspoon natural ground garlic powder
- 1/2 teaspoon Himalayan pink salt
- Other:
- 2 cups natural child bella mushrooms (de-stemmed, sliced)

- cup hand crafted almond milk

Directions:

1. Preheat oven to 425 degrees.
2. Set up the flavoring:
3. Add all ingredients for the flavoring to a little bowl and mix until all around joined. Change the flavors (cayenne pepper, garlic and salt) to your inclination. In the event that you don't need them too hot, simply utilize 1/4 teaspoon or less of cayenne pepper. Put away.
4. De-stem and cut the mushrooms. Put away.
5. Start a sequential construction system in a specific order: a) little bowl with sliced mushrooms b) little bowl with almond milk c) little bowl with 1/2 of the flavoring blend d) preparing container fixed with material paper
6. You should cover the mushrooms in (2) separate bunches, so start with (1) cup of the mushrooms and 1/2 of the flavoring blend.
7. Spot the (1) cup of mushrooms in the little bowl of milk, throw them around until they are completely covered, at that point utilizing a fork, remove them from the bowl of milk, let the abundance milk dribble off, and put them

in the bowl of preparing. Throw them around until they are totally covered with the flavoring blend. Move them onto the heating dish fixed with material paper and with your fork, delicately spread them out uniformly onto the container so they aren't covering or on top of one another.

a. Rehash Step 5 with the other (1) cup of mushrooms, utilizing a similar bowl of milk, and the other 1/2 of the flavoring combination.

8. Prepare at 425 degrees for 10 minutes.

9. Eliminate the container from the oven, and flip over the mushrooms so the opposite side can heat.

10. Return them to the oven for an extra 10 minutes.

11. Eliminate from oven and serve (they are best when served hot from the oven).

Appreciate!

15. Healthy Liver Cleanse Soup

Prep Time: 15 minutes Cook Time: 1 hour Total Time:1 hour 15 minutes Yields:4 servings

Ingredients:

- ▫ 3 cups water (separated/decontaminated)
- ▫ 1 cup natural vegetable stock
- ▫ 2 natural beets (stripped + diced)
- ▫ 2 natural carrots (sliced)
- ▫ 2 cups natural broccoli (chopped)
- ▫ 10 cloves natural garlic (newly squashed)
- ▫ 1 natural onion (diced)
- ▫ 1/2 natural lemon (newly pressed)
- ▫ 2 natural sound leaves
- ▫ 1/2 teaspoon Himalayan pink salt

- ▫ 1/2 teaspoon natural ground turmeric
- ▫ 1/2 teaspoon natural dried oregano
- ▫ 1/2 teaspoon natural ground dark pepper
- US Customary - Metric

Guidelines:

1. Set up the veggies:
2. Cut/Dice/Cut the beets, carrots, broccoli, and onions to the size of your inclination (see notes beneath).
3. Set up the soup:
4. Add every one of the ingredients for the soup to a medium-size pot and heat to the point of boiling.
5. Lower the warmth and stew on low warmth for roughly 60 minutes, or until the veggies are delicate.
6. Add additional water or veggie stock if necessary and change flavors to your inclination.

Formula Notes

1. Since this is a "liver purge" soup planned by Dr. Gathering to help detox your liver, you need to ensure you utilize unadulterated water

and natural ingredients to not bring new poisons into your body.

2. Veggies: Try to purchase natural ingredients to make this soup, if conceivable.

3. Water: Use clean, separated/sanitized water and not faucet water. I utilize a Berkey water channel framework for all my cooking.

4. Veggie Prep: Feel allowed to cut the veggies into whatever sizes you like, yet I dice the beets and onions, cut the carrots slight, and cut the broccoli into little scaled down pieces.

5. Veggie Broth: You may track down that the water + veggie stock level reductions as the soup is stewing. Provided that this is true, simply add extra veggie stock and change the flavors if necessary.

6. Lemon: It's ideal to utilize newly crushed natural lemon juice since it will contain the most supplements, yet you can utilize locally acquired natural lemon juice.

7. Garlic: Again, it's ideal to utilize newly squashed garlic rather than jostled garlic which contains additives.

8. Cove Leaves: Discard the narrows leaves when the soup is prepared and prior to serving.

9. Himalayan Pink Salt: This is the salt of my inclination, however you can generally substitute with ocean salt.

16. Healthy Gluten-Free Vegan Pumpkin Spice Cauliflower Rice Soup

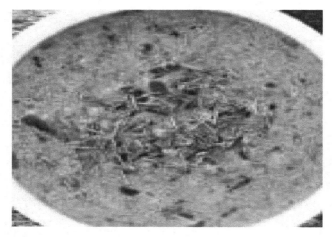

Prep Time: 10 minutes Cook Time: 5 minutes

Total Time:15 minutes Yields:4 servings

Ingredients:

- For the soup base:
- ▫ 1/2 cup natural red onion (diced)
- ▫ 1 clove natural garlic (newly squashed)
- ▫ 2 tablespoons 100% unadulterated avocado oil
- ▫ 1 teaspoon natural dried rosemary
- ▫ 1/2 teaspoon Himalayan pink salt
- ▫ 1/2 teaspoon natural ground dark pepper
- For the add-ins:
- ▫ 4 cups natural cauliflower rice

- ▫ 1 would organic be able to full-fat coconut milk (13.5-ounce can)
- ▫ 2 teaspoons natural pumpkin pie flavor

Directions:

1. Set up the soup base:
2. Add every one of the ingredients for the soup base to a non-poisonous skillet and saute' on medium warmth for around 2-3 minutes, or until the onions are delicate.
3. Add the add-ins:
4. Add the cauliflower rice, whole container of coconut milk and pumpkin flavor to the skillet and mix until very much consolidated.
5. Taste and change flavors to your inclination.
6. In the event that you are utilizing frozen cauliflower rice, stew on low-medium warmth until the cauliflower rice is defrosted and delicate
7. In the event that you are utilizing crude cauliflower, stew on low-medium warmth until the cauliflower rice is delicate.
8. Optional: Garnish with extra dried rosemary as well as ground dark pepper.
9. Best when served warm.

Formula Notes

1. Cauliflower Rice. You have two alternatives to browse for the cauliflower rice:

2. Frozen Cauliflower Rice - This is a helpful and modest choice. For instance, a 4-cup sack costs directly under $2.00 and I generally a few packs in my cooler consistently.

3. New Cauliflower Rice - You can make natively constructed cauliflower rice utilizing crude cauliflower. Essentially cut the cauliflower into reduced down floret pieces at that point beat in a food processor until it has the consistency of rice. Also, you should press any additional fluid from the rice prior to adding it to the formula.

4. Red Onion. I like to utilize the red onion assortment for the shading, yet don't hesitate to utilize your #1 assortment. Be that as it may, I would not suggest a sweet onion since this is an exquisite soup.

5. Avocado Oil. This can be subbed with natural extra-virgin olive oil in a similar sum.

6. Pumpkin Pie Spice. I like to utilize this great natural pumpkin pie zest. Be that as it may, don't hesitate to utilize whatever you have

close by and acclimate to add up to your inclination.

7. Dried Rosemary. I track down that dried rosemary turned out great however you could likewise utilize new rosemary for more serious flavor.

8. Coconut Milk. This is the thing that gives the soup a velvety surface. Ensure you use "full-fat" coconut milk and not "diminished fat" or "low-fat". What's more, ensure you buy canned coconut milk and not boxed.

9. While adding the coconut milk to the formula, you should add the whole can - coconut water and coconut fat.

10. Himalayan Pink Salt. This is my salt of inclination, nonetheless, it can generally be subbed with ocean salt. Utilize a 1/2 teaspoon to begin and add more on the off chance that you like.

17. Healthy Gluten-Free Vegan Flourless Pumpkin Spice Crackers with Sea Salt

prep 5 minscook 14 minstotal 19 mins

Ingredients

- For the wafers:
- 2 cups almond flour
- tablespoon 100% unadulterated avocado oil
- 1 flax egg (3 tablespoons separated water + 1 tablespoon natural ground flax)
- teaspoons natural pumpkin flavor
- 1/2 teaspoon Himalayan pink salt
- 1/4 teaspoon natural ground dark pepper

- 1/8 teaspoon natural ground garlic powder
- For the garnish:
- French Gray Sea Salt (or your #1 image)
- Basic Palate French Gray Sea Salt | The Healthy Family and Home

Directions:

1. Preheat oven to 350 degrees.
2. Set up the flax egg:
3. Add the ingredients for the flax egg (decontaminated/sifted water + ground flax) to a little bowl and race until it is all around consolidated. Put away.
4. Set up the wafers:
5. Add all ingredients for the wafers to a medium measured bowl and mix together until it is combined as one well.
6. Re-whisk the flax egg at that point add it to the bowl with the wafer ingredients and mix until everything is all around joined. Utilize a fork to squash the flax egg and avocado oil into the almond flour to ensure the almond flour is clammy. The blend ought to be brittle yet clammy.

7. Move the blend to a heating container fixed with material paper.

8. Utilizing your hands, structure the blend into a conservative ball shape, pressing it together firmly until it holds together well.

9. When you paint the town shape, place a second piece of material paper on top of the batter ball and carry it out level with a folding pin into a 1/4 inch thickness.

10. Utilize a pizza shaper or blade to cut the batter into little 1/2 x 1/2 inch squares. Try not to cut them any greater on the grounds that they won't hold together well. Eliminate the pieces and any morsels from the base piece of the material paper prior to preparing.

11. Sprinkle ocean salt over the highest point of the saltines and delicately tap the salt into the mixture so it doesn't tumble off when you flip them over later.

12. Prepare at 350 degrees for around 12-14 minutes, or until the edges and tops are somewhat brilliant. Flip the saltines over and heat for an extra 1-2 minutes, taking consideration not to consume them.

Store in an impermeable compartment.

Appreciate!

18. Healthy Gluten-Free Vegan Oven-Baked Okra Bites

Prep Time:10 minutes Cook Time:20 minutes

Total Time: 30 minutes

Ingredients:

- For the okra:
- ▫ 12 units natural okra (sliced)
- 2 tablespoons 100% unadulterated avocado oil (separated)
- For the bread pieces:
- 1/4 cup almond flour
- 1/4 cup dietary yeast*
- 1/4 teaspoon natural ground garlic powder
- 1/4 teaspoon natural ground cayenne pepper

- 1/4 teaspoon Himalayan pink salt
- US Customary - Metric

Directions:

1. Preheat oven to 425 degrees Fahrenheit.
2. Set up a treat sheet fixed with material paper, at that point put away.
3. Set up the bread pieces:
4. Add all ingredients for the bread pieces to a little bowl and mix until all around joined.
5. Taste and change the flavors to your inclination.
6. Set up the okra:
7. Cut the two closures off each piece of okra and dispose of. Cut the okra units into 1/4 inch cuts.
8. Move the okra cuts to a medium-size blending bowl.
9. Add 1 tablespoon avocado oil and throw with the okra cuts until it's equitably disseminated.
10. Add 1/2 of the bread scrap combination to the bowl of okra cuts and delicately throw until it's equitably conveyed and all pieces are covered.
11. Add the excess 1 tablespoon of avocado oil onto the breaded okra and delicately throw once

more, taking consideration to not shake off the current bread scrap covering.

12. Add the leftover 1/2 of the bread morsel combination and delicately throw once more, taking consideration not to shake off the current bread scrap covering.

13. Tenderly exchange the covered okra sliced to the readied treat sheet and prepare at 425 degrees Fahrenheit for 10 minutes.

14. Eliminate the heating skillet from the oven, flip over each piece and keep on preparing for an extra 10 minutes, or until they're brilliant earthy colored.

Best when served warm from the oven.

Formula Notes

1. Arrangement: The avocado oil and bread morsels will be isolated in this formula. You will throw the okra with the avocado oil then with the bread scraps once with the primary portion of the ingredients, at that point a second time with the second 50% of the ingredients. The

subsequent covering helps the breading stay the okra.

2. Okra: Fresh okra works best in this formula. Furthermore, cutting the okra into 1/4 inch pieces (not very thick and not very meager) will give the best outcomes.

3. Avocado Oil: I like to utilize avocado oil when preparing in the oven at high warmth, however you can substitute with natural extra-virgin olive oil.

4. *Nutritional Yeast: To make this formula 100% Medical Medium consistent, exclude the healthful yeast and substitute with extra flavors or utilize a natural chickpea bread scrap rather than the bread morsel combination recorded in the formula. In any case, you would have to run them through a Vitamix or food processor to make the surface better so they will adhere to the okra better.

5. Cayenne Pepper: I add this fixing to give the bread scraps a little hot flavor, yet it very well may be discarded or subbed with ground smoked paprika on the off chance that you don't care for zesty.

6. Himalayan Pink Salt. This is my salt of inclination, notwithstanding, it can generally be subbed with ocean salt.

7. Serving Size: This formula will make around (12) sliced cases of okra. Healthful data is for (3) sliced units which is (1) serving.

19. Healthy Gluten-Free Vegan Oven-Baked Sweet Potato "Toast" with Spicy Guacamole

Prep Time:5 minutes Cook Time:10 minutes

Total Time:15 minutes

Ingredients:

- For the yam "toast":
- ▫ 1 huge natural yam
- ▫ 1 teaspoon 100% unadulterated avocado oil
- For the guacamole:
- ▫ 2 natural avocados
- ▫ 1 tablespoon natural red onion (diced)
- ▫ 1 tablespoon natural new cilantro (chopped)
- ▫ 2 cloves natural garlic (newly squashed)

- □ 1 natural jalapeno* (diced)
- □ 1 teaspoon natural lime juice (newly pressed)
- □ 1-2 squeezes natural ground dark pepper
- □ 1/4 teaspoon Himalayan pink salt
- US Customary - Metric

Guidelines:

1. Preheat oven to 425 degrees Fahrenheit.
2. Set up a treat sheet fixed with material paper and put away.
3. Set up the yam "toast":
4. Wash and dry the yam.
5. Remove the two finishes of the yam.
6. Cut the yams start to finish in 1/4-inch thick pieces. You ought to have 4-6 cuts utilizing an enormous yam.
7. Spot the yam cuts on the readied treat sheet ensuring they don't cover.
8. Gently brush the two sides with avocado oil and daintily sprinkle with Himalayan pink salt.
9. Heat at 425 degrees for roughly 5 minutes. Flip the cuts over and keep preparing for an extra 5 minutes, or until they are completely cooked. They ought to be adequately delicate to stick a

fork through however strong enough to hold fixings.

10. Eliminate from the oven and get ready for gathering.
11. Set up the guacamole:
12. While the yam cuts are heating, set up the guacamole by adding all ingredients for the guacamole to a little bowl and crush it along with a fork until it gets to the consistency you like.
13. Taste and change the flavors to your inclination.
14. Gathering:
15. Move the yam cuts to your serving dish and top with 1-2 stacking tablespoons of guacamole.
16. Optional: Garnish with extra chopped cilantro as well as red onions.

Formula Notes

1. *Lectin-Free. Preclude the jalapeno to keep the formula 100% without lectin.
2. Yam. I suggest the "garnet" sweet potato assortment for best outcomes. Attempt to

track down the biggest and most uniform yam you can. Imagine the cuts you will make with the yam when choosing it. Likewise, there is no compelling reason to strip it - simply ensure the yam is cleaned and dried prior to heating. Remember that the size of the yam you use will decide the number of cuts it will yield. You ought to have the option to get between 4-6 cuts (at 1/4-inch thickness) from one huge yam.

3. Avocado Oil. This can be subbed with natural extra-virgin olive oil. Likewise, you would prefer not to utilize a lot on the yam cuts - just daintily brush some on each side.

4. Red Onion. I like to utilize red onions as a result of the shading it provides for the dish, yet you can utilize your number one onion assortment. Notwithstanding, I don't suggest sweet onions for this flavorful formula.

5. Cilantro. Continuously new, new, new! You may require some extra on the off chance that you need to decorate the yam toast prior to serving.

6. Garlic. Newly squashed garlic will give you the best flavor, however on the off chance that you

don't have any close by, you can likewise utilize natural ground garlic.

7. Jalapeno. I love to add jalapenos to my guacamole, however in the event that you don't care for zesty food sources or will serve this to youngsters, you might need to diminish or exclude the jalapenos.

8. Lime Juice. The newly crushed lime juice will give you the best flavor and dietary substance since it hasn't been purified, yet you can utilize natural locally acquired on the off chance that you don't have new limes.

9. Dark Pepper. I added this to upgrade the flavor profile, however it very well may be overlooked in the event that you like.

10. Himalayan Pink Salt. This is my salt of inclination, nonetheless, it can generally be subbed with ocean salt.

11. Serving Size: This formula will make roughly (4) cuts dependent on a huge yam. Wholesome data is determined for (2) cuts which is (1) serving dependent on a sum of (4) cuts. Remember you may get 4-6 cuts relying upon the size of the yam, so the dietary data could change.

20. Healthy Gluten-Free Vegan Oven-Baked Avocado Fries

prep 5 minscook 15 minstotal 20 mins

Ingredients:

- 2 natural avocados (firm, somewhat under ripe)
- 1/2 cup hand crafted almond milk
- For the bread pieces:
- 1/2 cup almond flour
- 1/2 cup dietary yeast
- 1/2 teaspoon natural ground garlic powder
- 1/2 teaspoon natural ground smoked paprika
- 1/2 teaspoon Himalayan pink salt
- Optional: For hot bread scraps, add 1/2 teaspoon natural ground cayenne pepper

Directions:

1. Preheat oven to 420 degrees.
2. Set up the bread scraps:
3. Add all ingredients for the bread pieces to a little bowl and mix until everything is all around consolidated. Change flavors to your inclination. Put away.
4. Set up the avocados:
5. It's significant that you have firm, marginally under ripe avocados for best outcomes. Soft or delicate avocados won't function admirably.
6. Cut the avocados down the middle and eliminate the pits.
7. Cautiously scoop out the avocados from the skins, and slice them through and through into 3-4 thick strips (contingent upon the size of your avocados). Put away.

Gathering:

1. Make a mechanical production system from left to right: a) plate with sliced avocado b) little bowl with non-dairy milk c) little bowl with

bread pieces d) heating container fixed with material paper.

2. Dunk every avocado cut into the bowl of milk, ensuring they are totally covered, at that point plunge the avocado cut into the bowl of bread scraps, ensuring they are totally covered on the two sides.

3. Spot the covered avocado cuts on the preparing dish fixed with material paper.

4. Prepare at 420 degrees for roughly 10 minutes, at that point turn them over and heat for an extra 5-10 minutes. Preparing times will differ however the outside of the avocado fries ought to be brilliant when prepared.

5. Present with your number one plunge or sauce and they are best when served hot from the oven.

Appreciate!

Conclusion

Hope you liked all recipes in this book .Alkaline diet carries many health benefits as well as these may also prove to be beneficial for people who want to lose weight.

CPSIA information can be obtained
at www.ICGtesting.com
Printed in the USA
BVHW092105240621
610373BV00002B/309